The Kingdom Within

John A. Sanford

Leader's Guide

HarperSanFrancisco
A Division of HarperCollins*Publishers*

Leader's Guide prepared by Loretta Girzaitis

THE KINGDOM WITHIN: *Leader's Guide.* Copyright © 1991 by HarperCollins. All rights reserved. Printed in the United States of America. No part of this book other than pages from the section "Materials for Group Distribution" may be used or reproduced in any manner whatsoever without written permission except in the case of brief quotations embodied in critical articles and reviews. Permission is granted to purchasers of this Leader's Guide to reproduce pages from the section "Materials for Group Distribution" for private or group use. For information address HarperCollins Publishers, Inc., 10 East 53rd Street, New York, NY 10022.

FIRST EDITION

Library of Congress Cataloging-in-Publication Data for original title
Sanford, John A.
    The kingdom within.
    Bibliography: p.
Includes index.
1. Jesus Christ—Words. I. Title.
BT306.S33   1987   232.9'54   86–45827
ISBN 0–06–067054–1

ISBN 0–06–067056–8 (Leader's Guide)

91 92 93 94 95 K.P. 10 9 8 7 6 5 4 3 2 1

Contents

Introduction	5
Starting an Adult Study Group and Using This Leader's Guide	6
Preparing for Session 1	9
Session 1 Getting to Know the Human Jesus	10
Session 2 What Is Jesus Saying?	16
Session 3 Are We Willing to Pay the Price?	21
Session 4 What Adversaries Block Our Path to God?	26
Session 5 How Can We Live Life to the Fullest?	33
Session 6 How Is Jesus Our Mentor?	39
Materials for Group Distribution	45
Glossary	46
Bibliography	49
Other Titles in Harper's Leader's Guide Series	71

Introduction

The Kingdom Within by John A. Sanford offers an opportunity for all to examine their inner world and discover the kingdom within that Jesus described. It is an examination of Jesus' sayings in order to delve deeper into their meaning for the unfolding of our personalities. When we begin to understand how these teachings affect us inwardly, they will guide us to a more conscious and creative outward life.

Sanford emphasizes that his book is only an interpretation and cautions that each of us must find our own meaning. "The teachings of Jesus are like a beautifully cut diamond," he says; "they can be viewed from many angles, yet each angle points to the same center" (p. 3).

So let us begin this adventure together, aware that we will need to listen to our own whisperings as well as to the insights of everyone within the group. We will need to take seriously the preparatory work we do ourselves and to trust that the Holy Spirit will be our guide as we meet. The purpose for our study is to acknowledge our inner world as a spiritual reality in order to develop a creative, personal relationship with God. The recognition that psychology and spirituality are interrelated is important.

The Kingdom Within: Leader's Guide

Starting an Adult Study Group and Using This Leader's Guide

Harper's series of Leader's Guides provides resources for small adult study groups. Each Guide is based on a widely read book by a well-known and knowledgeable author. Each provides suggestions for forming small groups and for leading the discussions. The Guides also provide discussion questions and other material that can be photocopied for participants.

Harper's Leader's Guides are designed for use in Christian churches of all denominations. However, they may also be used in other settings: neighborhood study groups, camps, retreat centers, colleges and seminaries, or continuing education classes.

Format

Harper's Leader's Guides have been planned as a basis for six one-hour sessions. Six weeks of discussion allows for depth and personal sharing, yet it is a limited commitment, one that busy adults find easier to make.

The Leader's Guides can be adapted for use in other time frames. By combining sessions, you can discuss a book in four meetings. Or, by being very selective with questions, you can plan a single two-hour session. The Guides can also serve as the foundation for a weekend retreat: the six hour-long sessions are alternated with recreation, rest, meals, and other activities.

Forming a Group

Choose a book that you think will be of interest to people in your congregation or other setting. Use your parish newsletter, announcements in services, visits to existing groups, and word of mouth to inform potential participants of the upcoming opportunity. It may be helpful to plan a brief orientation meeting for interested people.

Using This Leader's Guide

An effective discussion group can be formed with as few as three or four adults joined together by a common interest. If more than twelve people respond, they should probably be divided into smaller groups.

Participants should have access to the books at least a week before the first session. Books may be ordered through your local bookstore or from Customer Service, Harper San Francisco, 151 Union Street #401, San Francisco, CA 94111-1299, or call toll-free: 800–328–5125. Plan ahead and allow about six weeks for delivery.

At the time they receive their books, participants should also receive the material found at the back of this Leader's Guide: Materials for Group Distribution. You may photocopy this section to hand out. You may want to distribute all of the materials initially or you may distribute the information one session at a time.

Ask participants to take time to look these over before the session. The prepared discussion questions will serve as a medium to share insights, clarify questions, and reinforce learning.

Helps for Leaders

1. Be clear in announcing the time and place of the first meeting. If possible, choose a pleasant, comfortable room in which to meet where chairs can be set in a circle. This usually encourages more discussion than a formal classroom setting does.

2. Choose a leadership style: one person may lead the discussion in all six sessions, or there may be two people who co-lead every session or who alternate sessions. Leadership may also be rotated among the participants.

3. The Leader's Guide contains several kinds of questions. Some focus on what the book says. Do not neglect these; they are basic to intelligent discussion. These are also good questions for drawing more reluctant members into the discussion. Other questions deal more with the meaning and implications of the author's words. Still others ask participants to share experiences, ideas, and feelings of their own.

4. In the Leader's Guide you will find sample responses to questions. These are not to be considered the "right answers." They are only suggested responses, which often direct you to particular passages in the book. Be open to participants' responses that may stray from these suggested answers.

5. Materials for Group Distribution, found at the back of this Guide, can be photocopied for your group.

6. Don't feel that you have to "get through" all the questions and suggested activities in the Leader's Guide. Choose only those that seem most important to your group.

7. Try to avoid having one or two people monopolize the discussion. Call on some other participants to share their thoughts.

8. If the group spends too much time on one question, or if it goes off on a tangent, gently call it back to the topic by moving on to another question.

9. Encourage openness and trust in the group by being willing to share your own thoughts. Try to establish an atmosphere in which all ideas are treated with respect and seriousness.

10. The Leader's Guide contains some suggestions for group process. Experiment with these, and feel free to adapt them to your particular group.

Preparing for Session 1

Before the first session, invite participants to a brief meeting or send a letter of welcome to each registrant, identifying the location, date, and time of the session and asking each to read the introduction and chapter 1 of *The Kingdom Within*.

In the meeting or by mail, distribute the photocopied discussion guide for session 1, the glossary, and the bibliography. Encourage participants to respond to the discussion guide questions before the meeting because the success of the session will depend upon their participation. You may want to alert them that the questions are more personal than objective.

Invite participants to check the glossary for the Jungian terms that are unclear as they read *The Kingdom Within*. They can list the terms related to their readings that they would like better clarified during session 1. The bibliography is a reference for participants who are interested in reading one or several of the books as background material. You, too, may wish to do the same.

Make it clear that participants need to bring the book and handouts with them. You may want to provide a folder for each person upon arrival or suggest that they bring their own. You should remind participants that they will need to bring writing paper and pen or pencil to all sessions. They may find it helpful or convenient to keep a notebook in which they can record answers to discussion questions and take notes during each session.

Session 1: Getting to Know the Human Jesus

The Kingdom Within, introduction and chapter 1

Session Objectives
- To become acquainted with Jesus as an integrated and whole human being
- To recognize that Jesus is an important model for us
- To discover which aspects of our personalities need attention for integration and wholeness

Session Materials
- Copies of *The Kingdom Within* for newcomers
- Extra photocopies of the discussion guide for session 1, the glossary, and the bibliography
- Chalkboard and chalk; easel, newsprint, and pens; or an overhead projector with transparencies and pen
- Some New Testaments for looking up examples of Jesus' characteristics
- A comfortable and inviting environment (Have some plants and candles around. Light a candle, if not for the entire session, then at least for the closing prayer.)
- Photocopies of the closing for session 1 and the discussion guide for session 2 for each participant

Opening
Greet participants as they arrive. Provide name tags for this and several subsequent sessions until everyone knows the names of the others. Do not accept new members after this session because

catch-up work will be too difficult. If enough new people are interested in starting later, suggest that a new group be formed. Keep the group at ten or less; eight is an excellent number. With such a group, everyone can easily participate in the discussion and sharing. Begin and end on time.

To help participants get acquainted, ask them to give their names and to say something about themselves that will make them remembered by the group. However, feel free to use another method for introductions, if you wish. Also ask them to identify any expectations they have for the session. Begin the introductions with yourself and then go around the circle.

Guided Imagery Exercise:

Many adults have lost the art of creative imagination in the process of growing up. Yet so many of the things that exist today are the results of imagination: the light bulb, the spaceship, the computer. You can name many others.

It is not only the material world that depends upon imagination but also the inner world within us. There are many symbols in our unconscious that have messages for us and our task is to listen to them creatively.

Invite everyone to settle comfortably with their eyes closed and body relaxed, breathing deeply from the diaphragm. Then slowly read aloud the following exercise, pausing after each question to provide time for the imagery to surface.

Visualize yourself as a well. If you have never seen a well, create one in your imagination. (Pause) Where are you located? (Pause) How deep are you? (Pause) From where does the water come that is at the bottom of your well? (Pause) Who comes to your well to draw water? (Pause) Why is this water important for you? (Pause)

Now see yourself covered and abandoned. (Pause) How do you feel in this darkness? (Pause) Years go by and the source of your water dries up. How do you feel? (Pause) What needs to happen for you to become a well of life-giving water again? (Pause)

Give the group a few moments; ask all to open their eyes when they have finished their visualization. Then invite those who wish to share what the image was and how they felt as they were visualizing their well.

Ask all to draw the well they imagined, when they get home, and to color it in whatever way they wish. Request that they write their insights and feelings below their picture or on the back of it. Emphasize the importance of their keeping this picture until the end, for they will return to this image during the last session.

Reflecting Together

Chapter 1: The Personality of Jesus

Ask each person to identify the terms in chapter 1 that are unclear to them and make sure that these are clarified, for they will be referred to in future sessions.

Make sure that you are familiar with the terms yourself by studying the glossary or other references before the session. If someone raises terms that are not listed, inquire whether anyone in the group can clarify them. If not, look them up later or get a volunteer to do so and be prepared to deal with them at the beginning of the next session.

Terms that might need clarifying include: archetype, attitude, conscious, dreams, ego, ego strength, extravert, feeling, feminine aspect, function, introvert, intuition, masculine aspect, numinous, perceiving, Self, sensation, thinking, unconscious.

Once this has been accomplished, discuss the questions in the discussion guide for chapter 1, which are given below along with suggested answers. Most of the questions, however, are personal applications, so the responses will be varied.

Since group members should have reflected on these questions before the session, invite them to begin the sharing as you ask the questions. Be as informal as you can, with anyone joining the discussion whenever he or she wishes. Do not force anyone to participate, since responses will be touching their innermost selves.

Session 1

Do not feel obligated to cover all the questions. Choose those which you sense have the most meaning for your group.

Remember to allow ten minutes for the closing activity.

1. Identify the behavior within yourself that is extravert and introvert. Which predominates? What might be needed to bring a better balance to your life?

Anwers will vary. Go over Sanford's explanation of these categories (p. 16) if necessary.

2. In light of what you know of Jesus, identify his extravert and introvert characteristics. What do these characteristics say about Jesus?

As these are identified, list them in separate columns on the chalkboard, easel, or overhead.

3. Do you feel you need to become better acquainted with Jesus? If so, how? Journal about the specific ways you can do this.

If anyone is not familiar with journaling, take a few moments to explain how this is done.

4. How was Jesus a thinking person, one who dealt with situations through abstract thought, arriving logically at a conclusion?

Sanford explains it this way: "The thinking function of Jesus is seen in his intellectual bouts with the Pharisees, and in his astuteness. When confronted with a situation that called for quick logical analysis, for objective and keen thought, Jesus met the challenge with ease, a sign that he was well-developed as a thinking person" (p. 20). See also the specific Gospel references Sanford gives on page 20.

5. How was Jesus a feeling person, one who saw the value in a situation and then acted with compassion rather than judgment?

Sanford gives specific examples on pages 20 to 21. Have participants look them up, if necessary.

6. How was Jesus a sensate person, aware of facts through the senses and very practical about life?

Sanford talks about Jesus' "acute awareness of the facts of the world in which he lived" (p. 19). Ask participants to come up with examples (see pp. 19–20).

7. How was Jesus an intuitive person, perceiving the subtle aspects of a relationship and of the possibilities in life?

If group members cannot come up with concrete examples, refer to the passages Sanford cites (p. 20).

Always close your discussion period with your own observations about the process, the participation, or the insights which surfaced.

Looking Ahead

Announce the time and place of the next meeting. Ask participants to read chapters 2 and 3 of *The Kingdom Within* and to answer the questions in the discussion guide for session 2. Distribute the discussion guides at this time.

Invite all to choose one of the images of the kingdom identified in these chapters and to journal about its personal meaning for them. Let them know that they will introduce themselves at the next session by identifying an image and its significance for them.

Encourage them to journal also about the means by which they can get to know Jesus better.

Request that each bring a Bible to the next meeting. Bibles do not need to be of the same translation; in fact, a different translation may help to clarify an obscure passage.

Closing

At this time, ask everyone to call out a word or phrase identifying their feelings about the session. Do not make any comments about these. Light your candle if it has not been lit during the session.

Begin with the closing prayer for session 1 found on the handout, to be distributed at this time. Then invite those who wish to offer a spontaneous prayer of petition, praise, or thanksgiving.

Do not wait for *everyone* to pray, but when you judge that no more prayers will be said out loud, close this period by offering everyone's prayers, saying "God, we offer you our prayers, spoken and unspoken, and trust that you will bless us with your love." Then ask everyone to stand for the blessing.

Ask each person to turn to the person on his or her right and say "May God bless you and your family" or something similar, making the sign of the cross or holding the person's shoulders or hands. Model this blessing by being the first one to do it.

After the blessing, dismiss everyone graciously. Invite anyone with questions to feel free to speak to you.

Session 2: What Is Jesus Saying?

The Kingdom Within, chapters 2 and 3

Session Objectives

- To focus on some key statements Jesus made on the kingdom
- To recognize the difference between the "Law and the Prophets" and the "law of Love"

Session Materials

- Extra photocopies of the discussion guide for session 2
- Several copies of the Bible for those who may have forgotten to bring one
- A candle to use at the time of the closing prayer (It may be lit during the entire session.)
- Photocopies of the closing for session 2 and the discussion guide for session 3 for each participant

Opening

This session covers chapters 2 and 3 of *The Kingdom Within*. Before formally beginning the session, review the terms conscious and unconscious.

At the end of session 1 all participants were asked to take one of the kingdom images and journal about its application to their lives. Start the session by inviting those comfortable with doing so to share what they have written or the insights they received as they were writing. Take about ten minutes for this.

Reflecting Together

It may not be possible to discuss all of the questions on the handout due to the time limit. Some are personal, some objective. Review the questions before the session and check off those that you feel are most helpful to your group, so you can be sure to cover them.

Choose those that foster internalization and provide others with insights they might not otherwise have. You may need to give more time to Chapter 2 than Chapter 3; use your discretion. Remember to allow ten minutes for closing and prayer.

Chapter 2: The Treasure of the Kingdom of God

1. What is the treasure hidden within the field of your soul (Matt. 13:44)? What are you willing to give up to possess it? How are you a pearl found by the kingdom of God (Matt. 13:45–46)?

> Answers will vary. Allow time for a couple of personal answers, and any interesting thoughts on the difference between the treasure and the pearl.

2. Searching and being sought are ongoing experiences and imply a continuing transformation of attitudes, values, and character. Draw a spiritual timeline and on it, identify the moments when such changes occurred in your life. Such a timeline highlights those periods in your life when some significant movement took place. Include those movements also where it seemed you may have backtracked or even moved away from God. Does any pattern emerge?

> You may ask who drew a timeline and what insights they got from it. Those who wish to could pair up sometime during the week to go over their timelines together in detail.

3. What does "being born again" (John 3:3) mean to you? How do you feel about Jesus' invitation to you for a special personal relationship with God?

> Answers will vary.

4. Do you agree with the following statements? Indicate why or why not.

> A. Only the person who leads his or her life by an individually worked out set of values based on self-knowledge can enter the kingdom of God (Matt. 5:20).
>
> B. Lying within our shadow is the possibility of murder, adultery, stealing, lying, and coveting. For this reason the Law is necessary.
>
> C. When we confront and deal with the above possibilities, then we can live in love and transcend the Law (Matt. 5:17–18; Luke 16:17).
>
> D. When we obey the Law, we are better than prostitutes, murderers, drug addicts, alcoholics (Matt. 21:31).
>
> Answers will vary for each statement. Invite participants to give examples from contemporary life.

5. In one column list your inner values and in another your outer values (pp. 37–39). Then examine which rule your life and how these values support or negate one another. What do these insights say to you?

> Answers will vary.

6. How does "understanding" the kingdom affect your life on earth? What does it promise after death? How do the present and future relate?

> Sanford points out that, while we experience the kingdom and its rewards in this life, we don't exactly understand what it means in the life after death. "But if life has a meaning, so does death; and if we become whole, something indestructible is forged in us that, in ways that pass our understanding, joins us to the fabric of eternal life. This is the ultimate promise of the kingdom of God" (p. 41).

Session 2

Chapter 3: Entering into the Kingdom

1. **What does the saying "Many are called but few are chosen" (Matt. 22:14) mean to you? Would you consider yourself called and chosen or called and not chosen? Why must this be an individual decision?**

    Answers will vary.

2. **Why do you agree or disagree with Sanford's statement that "people hate and fear individuality, with its demands for freedom and consciousness, and so they reject the kingdom of God" (p. 45)?**

    In discussing this statement, you may want to consider the larger context Sanford gives it on page 45.

3. **As you look at your life at this time, do you feel you are self-sufficient and can manage your life easily, or do you find yourself wounded, floundering, dissatisfied? Give an example from your experience to support your feeling. What do you need to do during this stage in your life?**

    Answers will vary.

4. **Jesus said that people do not put new wine into old wineskins (Matt. 9:17; Mark 2:22; Luke 5:37–39). In your life, what corresponds to the old wineskin? the new wine? the new, fresh wineskin?**

    Answers will vary.

5. **Visualize the story of the storm at sea as told in Luke 8:22–25. Think of an experience of yours that you connect with a storm at sea (or a hurricane), thunderous clouds (or driving rain), or an earthquake or tornado. Draw a picture of this symbol or write a poem connecting the symbol with your experience.**

    Ask one or two people to share their drawings or poems. Encourage everyone to do this exercise at home, if they haven't done it for this session.

The Kingdom Within: Leader's Guide

6. Choose one of these New Testament passages and write a short description of how it applies to your life: the narrow gate (Matt. 7:13); losing one's life (Matt. 10:31); the invitation to the wedding (Matt. 22:1–10; Luke 14:16–24); the house built on a rock (Matt. 7:24–25; Luke 6:47–48); or, "Who do you say I am?" (Matt. 16:13–20).

Encourage the group to focus on others of these passages at some later date, especially when an event in their lives triggers a need.

As you end the discussion, invite feedback about the process, time limitations, or other concerns anyone might have. Keep this short, however, mindful that you need to bring the session to a close.

Looking Ahead

Pass out the discussion guide for session 3 and ask participants to read chapters 4 and 5 of *The Kingdom Within* and to respond to the questions. They will need to bring their Bibles and their folders to the next session.

Closing

Distribute the closing prayer for session 2 and read together. Again, allow time for petitions and prayers of thanksgiving. You may choose some response the group will use for these prayers, such as "Lord, hear us," or "Lord, we trust you." Those who do not wish to offer prayers may share an insight for which they are grateful. Invite everyone to express some symbol of acceptance to each other, such as a handshake or a hug.

Session 3: Are We Willing to Pay the Price?

The Kingdom Within, chapters 4 and 5

Session Objectives

- To examine the requirements of discipleship
- To recognize the ways we use masks when we are afraid to be ourselves

Session Materials

- Extra photocopies of the discussion guide for session 3
- Several Bibles
- A candle to use at the time of the closing prayer (It may be lit during the entire session.)
- Photocopies of the closing for session 3 and the discussion guide for session 4 for each participant

Opening

Invite participants to share some significant event that occurred in their lives since the group last met. Do not take too long for this; a simple statement is enough.

Reflecting Together

This session covers chapters 4 and 5. Review the new terms participants met with in their preparation which are not yet clearly understood.

The Kingdom Within: Leader's Guide

Chapter 4: The Price of Discipleship

This may be a difficult session, since the sayings of Jesus chosen for it are hard ones. Keep the discussion moving, yet be sensitive enough to recognize the need for staying with a particular question if the participants need the time. Let the discussion flow according to the needs and interests of the group.

1. Sanford uses two New Testament images of Christ as the Word, one as a sword that divides and separates and the other as fire which burns and purifies (pp. 58–59). How relevant are these images to your life?

Answers will vary. Have participants think about how they react to Jesus' teachings that he has come to set family members against one another (Matt. 10:35–36) and that none can be his disciples unless they hate members of their own household (Luke 14:25–26).

2. If you have separated from family identification, either inwardly or outwardly, how was this accomplished? Do you feel anything more has to be done?

After one or two participants have given their answers to this question, lead the group in talking about what risks are involved in choosing the kingdom over family and friends. Ask them what they felt as they thought and wrote about this.

3. Do you agree or disagree that our following of Christ aids us in establishing true relationships with others?

As they answer, have participants reconcile this idea with the idea that when Christ calls us to be his followers, we need to sacrifice our loyalty to family, country, church and discuss the conflicts that surface.

4. Sanford says, "The kingdom is not obedience, but creativity" (p. 66). What does this mean to you?

Answers will vary. You might go around the room, having participants give one-word examples of the creativity of the kingdom.

5. Jesus tells us that his yoke is easy and his burden light (Matt. 11:29–30) and he challenges us to accept both. Have you found this to be true in your experience? Why or why not?

Answers will vary.

6. Sanford emphasizes the need to move away from the group to foster individuality. What modern institutions and impulses contradict this? How do you deal with the apparent contradiction?

Discuss whether Sanford is implying that AA, Cursillo, Marriage Encounter, Bible study, faith sharing, and support groups of various kinds harm us. Robert Bellah in his book *Habits of the Heart* condemns individualism and emphasizes the need for the community. How are these perspectives reconcilable—or aren't they? Be prepared for group participants to disagree with each other.

Chapter 5: The Pharisee in Each of Us

1. Recall a time when you wore your mask in a healthy way; in an unhealthy way.

After people give their personal examples, ask: What would be involved for you to be yourself at all times—to have appearances and reality agree?

2. Make two lists—one list for sins of the spirit, the other for sins of the flesh.

Break the group up into groups of three and allow ten minutes for them to share their lists with one another, identifying why they placed each example where they did. When everyone regroups, ask: 1) Was there anything with which you strongly disagreed? 2) What did you hear that affected your understanding?

3. **When have you acted as a "Pharisee"? What can you do to take your "heart" seriously?**
Answers will vary. Refer participants to the glossary for "Pharisees" and "heart."

4. **Read Psalm 139:1–18, then write your own paraphrase of it. You might want to use the paraphrase in the handout as a model.**
Ask participants to read to each other their paraphrases in groups of two. Ask for one or two volunteers to read theirs during the closing.

5. **What is the ethic of the kingdom? What is the reality of living it out like for you?**
"One who seeks the kingdom of God cannot put worldly goals ahead of spiritual goals" (p. 75). Read Matthew 22:21 together and talk about when these commitments have created conflicts.

6. **Does Jesus condemn wealth in itself? How can wealth be an obstacle to the kingdom of God?**
"The danger of wealth is not that it automatically excludes the one who possesses it from the kingdom, but that it greatly strengthens the outer mask and inflates the ego" (p. 76). Discuss the ways in which wealth inflates the ego.

7. **What does nakedness in dreams have to do with the nakedness in the Garden of Eden? What do you think of the quotation on page 78 from the Gospel According to Thomas?**
Sanford writes: "In our dreams the loss of the mask is sometimes represented as nakedness" (p. 78). Let participants talk about their own relevant dreams.

8. **At this time in your life, how can you shed your mask, that**

is, confront something in yourself that you do not like, even if it is unpleasant for you?

Answers will vary.

Suggest to participants that they might benefit by doing some dream journaling as suggested on their handout for this session.

Looking Ahead

Pass out the handouts for the next session and ask participants to read chapters 6 and 7 of *The Kingdom Within* and to respond to the questions. Encourage them to continue journaling about the insights they have gained during the past three sessions.

Ask anyone in the group who has a guitar to bring it to the next session, or use a piano or organ if there is one in the meeting area. Let the group choose a hymn or a song that everyone knows to sing at the end of the next session. If no instrument is available, sing anyway, without accompaniment.

Closing

This session may have been a disturbing one to some, since it presented difficult concepts. The Gospel selections that were used are those that many bypass or ignore. Some may resist accepting the Gospel challenge because it is so different from cultural, societal, or family norms.

Be sensitive to this. At the end of this session, allow people to express their feelings without any comment. Be as vulnerable yourself as you expect them to be.

Light the candle if it has not been lit. Distribute the closing prayer for session 3. Before using the paraphrase of Psalm 139 found in the handout, have someone read the Psalm from the Bible. Then read the paraphrase together. Afterwards, invite those who wish to read their own paraphrases to do so. Watch the time, however.

To close, stand and form a circle. As everyone holds hands, recite the Lord's Prayer together.

Session 4: What Adversaries Block Our Path to God?

The Kingdom Within, chapters 6 and 7

Session Objectives
- To recognize and acknowledge the enemy within us
- To examine the power of evil and sin in our lives

Session Materials
- Extra photocopies of the discussion guide for session 4
- Several Bibles
- Chalkboard and chalk, poster paper and marker, or an overhead projector
- A candle to use at the time of the closing prayer (It may be lit throughout the session.)
- Photocopies of the discussion guide for session 5 for each participant

Opening

Ask participants to share something they consider evil, whether this is something they have themselves experienced or something they have noticed in society, business, church, etc. Ask them to make a simple statement without elaboration.

Clarify whatever new words in chapters 6 and 7 still seem unclear.

Reflecting Together

This session covers chapters 6 and 7 of *The Kingdom Within*, which may be somewhat complex and perplexing, yet are important

Session 4

chapters. If there are different perceptions about evil and sin within the group, be patient. Encourage each participant to listen and to test what is heard against personal understandings and values.

Chapter 6: The Inner Adversary

1. What kind of self-image do you have? How was it formed? What would happen to you if it were to change?

Ask several participants to say what would happen to them if their self-image changed.

2. When are you aware of your inner adversary (p. 82)? How do you feel when it surfaces? What happens when you don't deal with it?

Sanford writes, "The more we are identified with a mask, the more the unconscious will set up an opposing viewpoint in the form of the inner enemy. The more we pretend to be this or that, the more the enemy will be the opposite. Therefore, it is only as we become conscious of the mask we wear that we can hope to make peace with ourselves" (p. 83).

3. What happens when you identify and acknowledge the inner enemy as your own?

"The recognition of the inner enemy . . . causes us to relinquish an identification with our mask and to accept our reality as a person . . . . The inner enemy includes essential parts of ourselves [and] now they can be included in the conscious personality instead of being relegated to the hell of being split off in the unconscious" (p. 85).

4. Do you agree with Sanford when he interprets the parable of the prodigal son as evidence of the two sides of our personalities (pp. 87–88)?

If necessary, reread Sanford's interpretation on pages 87 to 88 as a group. Talk about why some participants agree or disagree with Sanford.

5. Can you identify any projections (p. 84) you have placed on others? What are the consequences both for you and for the other when this is done?

Have the group look at Sanford's examples on page 84, and give their own personal examples.

6. Make a list of your enemies. Alongside each name write down what you would need to do to make them your friends.

Ask the groups: What were your feelings as you answered this question? How and when can you put into action what needs to be done to love your neighbor?

7. Rate yourself from 1 (not true) to 5 (true) on the inventory below by circling the number that applies for each statement. If you feel that some areas are important and need more attention, what steps can you take to make the statement a reality?

This inventory is personal and will not need to be shared with the group unless you care to identify some decision you are making because of the insights you gained as you did the inventory.

> **A. I know and accept myself because I recognize that my past has shaped me into who I am today.**
>
> 1   2   3   4   5
>
> **B. I acknowledge and embrace my inner enemy (shadow).**
>
> 1   2   3   4   5
>
> **C. I identify and claim both my negative and positive feelings.**
>
> 1   2   3   4   5
>
> **D. I live according to my inner values rather than those imposed from the outside.**
>
> 1   2   3   4   5

Session 4

E. I trust my intuition and God's grace that I can be "perfect," that I can become the person God has created me to become.

1   2   3   4   5

F. I believe that the kingdom can be established in me because my faults and failures contribute to developing my potential and capacity for love.

1   2   3   4   5

Individuals are free to share their insights, but should not be pushed to do so.

Chapter 7: The Role of Evil and Sin in the Way

1. Have you personally experienced crises that made you ask "Why"? Do you believe that evil experiences are allowed by the "dark side of God" (p. 103) so persons might achieve inner strength and courage?

As participants give their personal experiences, ask: "What have such experiences done to you?"

2. Evil exists when something is not what it is meant to be. Since we are not whole (what we are meant to be), we are the prey of evil and so can possibly choose against God (p. 103). ✓ Identify as many areas of evil as you can: in the world; in others; in yourself.

Some possible answers: power and wealth inordinately used; success which becomes a god; manipulation of people and countries; ruthlessness; forcing others into a mold; not living up to one's potential.

As participants suggest answers, write them on the chalkboard, poster paper, or overhead projector.

3. Why is the ego important?

"It is the task of the ego to become conscious of the two sides of the Self and through this act of consciousness to heal the

The Kingdom Within: Leader's Guide

split" (p. 101). "Without an ego there can be no personality, nor can there be a recognition of God, so the ego is very necessary to God as well as to human beings" (p. 109). If necessary read what Sanford has to say about the ego on pages 108 to 109.

4. Sanford claims that the higher morality of love exceeds that of the Law, leading to a confrontation with this enemy (pp. 111–12). Would you be able to live without the Law and reach this higher plane? Why or why not?

Answers will vary. Sanford states that we need the commandments because we are egocentric, have an enemy within us, do covet, have adulterous urges. Have participants discuss how this applies to them.

5. As you read the following statements, circle the letters (from strongly disagree to strongly agree) which identify your stance.

    A. Guilt is healthy when it makes us conscious of our sinful behavior.

    SD   D   N   A   SA

    B. It is necessary for us to be forgiven much, if we are to love much.

    SD   D   N   A   SA

    C. If we are to be united with God, we must drop our mask and consciously confront our inner enemy.

    SD   D   N   A   SA

    D. Sin is living unconsciously and when in sin it is not possible to make a free choice; we are thus enslaved to what we don't know about ourselves.

    SD   D   N   A   SA

E. Only through consciousness can our inner divisions be brought within God's healing power.

SD   D   N   A   SA

Have people share their responses in groups of three.

6. Write two haiku poems—one on evil and one on sin. Haiku is a three-line poem with five syllables in the first line, seven in the second line, and five in the third line. Two poems are given as models.

EVIL

The demon within
Defies God, claims my spirit,
Makes itself my friend.

SIN

Darkness floods my heart.
I flounder, lost in a maze,
Choose what pleases me.

Ask participants to read their haiku to the group.

Looking Ahead

Tie up any loose ends from the session's discussion. Then pass out the handouts for session 5 and ask the group to read chapters 8 and 9 of *The Kingdom Within*. Ask them to choose one of the biblical verses that says something special to them as they read these two chapters. Tell them to form a short prayer or reflection (two or three sentences) to share in the closing at the next session.

Closing

Light the candle, if it has not been lit. Invite everyone into a circle and ask one person to read Matthew 22:37–39. Invite the participants to say a short spontaneous prayer either praising, thanking, or petitioning God in relation to what was heard. You may want to model the prayer yourself by saying "Lord, I accept this commandment and thank you for it. Give me the grace to live it." Ask those who do not wish to offer a prayer just to express their gratitude for something.

Close the session with the hymn or song the group chose at its last session.

Session 5: How Can We Live Life to the Fullest?

The Kingdom Within, chapters 8 and 9

Session Objectives

- To understand that the body and soul are a unity which cannot be fragmented nor ignored
- To examine the role of the opposites within our unconscious

Session Materials

- Extra photocopies of the discussion guide for session 5
- A candle to use at the time of the closing prayer (It may be lit during the session.)
- Photocopies of the discussion guide for session 6 for each participant

Opening

Invite the participants to read their haiku poems out loud again to start off the session. Allow some silence for reflection after each haiku.

Discuss any new terms that are still unclear.

Reflecting Together

This session can be a difficult one if it is not handled in a sensitive manner. The participants should have a high trust level by now, because they have been sharing some deeply personal insights in the past sessions, but if anyone is reticent about participating, do not prod. Remember that listening is just as important as speaking.

Chapter 8: The Faith of the Soul

1. Jesus was capable of lasting, deep personal relationships because his eros (p. 123) was well developed. How are your relationships in light of your eros?

Answers will vary. Go over Sanford's explanation of eros on page 123, if necessary.

2. When Jesus speaks of faith, he is speaking of a certain capacity to affirm life in spite of what negatives life may bring. Is your faith deep enough to live life to its fullest?

Answers will vary. Ask participants to give examples of faith at work.

3. Jesus asks "what does it profit a man if he gains the whole world and loses his soul." What would you be willing to give up to save your soul?

See Sanford's discussion of Matthew 16:26, Mark 8:36, and Luke 9:25 on page 126.

4. How conscious are you of your body, with its instincts and emotions? Do you honor, love, and care for it, or do you ignore, subdue, and/or chastise it?

Answers will vary.

5. How conscious are you of your soul, that reality that makes you alive from within? How do you nurture your relationship with it?

Answers will vary. Ask for examples of how various participants nurture this relationship.

6. Write a letter to a person of the opposite sex in which you explain your feelings and values about these elements:

    A. the proper balance between repressing your sexuality and living it out promiscuously;

Session 5

B. the difference between the real person in your sexual life and the ideal person of your fantasies. What role does projection play in the latter?;

C. the motivation(s) for a sexual experience with someone;

D. the message that sexual fantasies have for you.

You are writing this letter simply to clarify for yourself what your attitudes are about your own and others' bodies. There is no need to share this letter, unless you wish.

You may want to make reference to this letter by asking how many wrote it; how they felt while writing it; what insights it provided. If there are several who did not write it, you might ask them why they did not do so. However, be careful not to pry.

7. Do you agree that sexual sins are not as serious as hypocrisy, deceit, self-righteousness, egocentricity (p.130)? Why or why not?

Sanford points out: "There is not one single phrase from the lips of Jesus in condemnation of the instinctual side" (p. 130). Allow people to express their feelings about this statement.

8. How conscious are you of your sexuality (your maleness or femaleness)? How and when do you express it and how does it affirm physical love and your respect for the other?

Answers will vary.

Chapter 9: The Lost Coin

1. Identify what you fear the most within yourself that you resist bringing into the light. How can you overcome this resistance?

Answers will vary. Bring up Sanford's points about our unconscious on page 137: Our unredeemed humanity is found in our unconscious. Because it seems objectionable, inferior or unwanted, we fear to bring all of it into consciousness. But unless we do, we will not discover the kingdom within us.

2. In separate columns list the characteristics that you consider masculine and feminine. Put a check mark next to each characteristic that you feel is part of your personality.

Have people look at their lists and ask themselves these questions: Is there a balance or are you top-heavy in one or the other? Are you satisfied with this? Do you need to correct an imbalance?

Now is also a good time to review the characteristics of Jesus' personality examined in session 1, having people apply them to themselves to see how balanced and integrated they are. Direct participants: Just as you examined your masculine/feminine traits, do the same with these two pairs: thinking/feeling; sensation/intuition. Be sure to think about what action(s) you will take if you perceive an imbalance.

3. In order to become a totally integrated and redeemed person, you need to find the lost sheep within you (Matt. 18:12–14; Luke 15:4–7). Who is your lost sheep?

"Psychologically, the one lost sheep represents the lost part of ourselves, the part of our total personality that is submerged in the depths, caught in the hell of our inner separation, and that must be recognized and brought into expression if we are to be complete" (p. 143). Have participants give specific examples of what part of themselves they have lost.

4. In the parable of the lost coin (which is also the lost part of ourselves) we need to "light a lamp" (Luke 15:8–9) if we are to find that which is lost. On what do you need to shed the light of your mind and heart in order to search for and find your lost coin?

Session 5

Answers will vary. Ask people to compare their answers to this question and question 3.

5. Jesus said, "I was hungry and you gave me food; I was thirsty and you gave me drink; I was a stranger and you made me welcome; naked and you clothed me, sick and you visited me, in prison and you came to see me. . . . I tell you solemnly, in so far as you did this to one of the least of these brothers of mine, you did it to me" (Matt. 25:35–36, 40). What is the naked, needy, hungry part of you that needs to be cared for? How can this inner beggar save you?

Answers will vary. Read Sanford's stories on page 145.

6. What sets us into position for receiving the kingdom of God?

"With the removal of the hubris of the ego [the insolence and arrogance caused by inordinate pride] and the inclusion of the inferior, hitherto unconscious parts of our personality that our connection to the soul has made possible, we are now in a position to receive the kingdom of God" (p. 148).

Looking Ahead

Draw attention to the fact that there is only one more session. Remind the group to read chapter 10 and the conclusion to *The Kingdom Within*. Distribute the handouts. Also ask them to bring in the drawings they made of the well they visualized in the first session. They will use these for the opening when they share their "well" and "water" in light of the growth that has taken place during these past sessions.

Review the meaning of symbol and invite them to bring one that would express where they are right now in relation to the kingdom of God. It could be a pearl, a fish, a stone, a heart, a bird, a picture, etc. Tell them this will be part of the next session's closing when they will display their symbols and explain their meanings to the group.

Closing

Light the candle if it has not been lit. Invite all to form a circle and to share the prayer or reflection they composed based on the biblical verse they chose from either chapter 8 or 9. End with some expression of friendship, such as a handshake, a hug, or a blessing.

Session 6: How Is Jesus Our Mentor?

The Kingdom Within, chapter 10 and conclusion

Session Objectives

- To examine the steps that need to be taken to live out the kingdom
- To examine the ways we can use Jesus as a prototype for ourselves

Session Materials

- Extra photocopies of the discussion guide for session 6
- Photocopies of the supplementary handout "Continuing the Learning" for each participant
- A seasonally decorated table with space for the symbols which everyone will bring and a separate area upon which to place the drawings of the well after these have been explained

Opening

This opening may take a little longer than usual, but it is important. Ask each person to explain their drawing of the well and how its image may have changed since the first session. This can give the group some clue about the ongoing growth possible in life. Have everyone place the drawing in the area you have designated for it. Encourage the participants to examine these wells during the break.

Reflecting Together

This is the final meeting of the group and it is meant to put the six sessions into perspective. Help individuals synthesize the experiences and insights of their time together.

The Kingdom Within: Leader's Guide

Chapter 10: The Coming of the Kingdom

1. The kingdom is established in our inner center when we surrender our ego to its supremacy. The paradox is that in this surrender the ego is strengthened and so becomes representative of our total personality. Read the sayings of Jesus in Matthew 10:39 and 23:12. Have you ever experienced this paradox in your outer life of commitment, or your inner life of surrender? If so, what resulted?

Answers will vary.

2. How does surrender differ from weakness?

"[It would be weakness] to extinguish, nullify, or devalue the ego. The position of the ego in the total personality is one of extreme importance. There can be no wholeness, no strength, no capacity to be used by God without a strong ego. It is only an ego made strong by inner confrontation that is capable of performing the act of self-sacrifice. A weak ego feels compelled to fight and struggle for its very existence. Out of fear the weak ego will defend itself against life and the inner world by means of an assortment of egocentric defenses and attitudes that prevent it from turning itself over to be used by the kingdom.

"We cannot sacrifice what we do not have. If we are not in possession of ourselves we cannot turn ourselves over to God for his use" (pp. 149–50).

3. Who are the poor in spirit? When do you see yourself as self-sufficient? as poor in spirit?

"The 'poor in spirit' are those who recognize that they must beg for their spirit from a source beyond themselves. Such people find the kingdom, while those who regard themselves as self-sufficient do not receive the highest gift" (p. 150). Some participants might want to share anecdotes of their own illustrating this difference.

Session 6

4. When are you childish (dependent, regressive, infantile)? When are you childlike (creative, spontaneous, free of inhibitions, generating new life)?

Answers will vary. As the leader, give your own answer to make it easier for others to give theirs.

5. Read Isaiah 11:6–8. What is the wolf in you? the lamb? the panther? the kid? How can you take the hostile elements and make them friends with the gentle ones? How are you the little boy or little girl who leads them?

Read Isaish 11:6–8 as a group before you discuss individual answers to this question.

6. How prepared are you for your inner wedding (that union with Christ that brings freedom from evil because it is uniting the opposites within you [p. 153])?

Discuss Sanford's interpretation of the kingdom as wedding on pages 153 to 154 as an introduction to talking about how prepared individual participants are.

7. Why is it necessary that our inner journey be lifelong?

"No human being ever reaches the end of his or her inner journey; for, as the kingdom begins to become a reality within, there is generated from within a host of new possibilities that consciousness can fulfill. So the life of the kingdom is dynamic and continually evolving" (p. 157).

8. What connections can you make between creativity and fish?

"Fish are a favorite symbol in our dreams for contents of the inner world. Fish lurk under the surface; they may be abundant, but they are hard to see. However, they may be caught by patience and skill, and when they are caught they may be eaten and so taken into oneself. The contents of the inner world are also below the surface. They too may be lifted up into consciousness and taken as food for our lives" (pp. 157–158).

Use Sanford's points as a jumping-off point for connecting fish with creativity. Allow the group to make unusual comparisons.

The following section concludes the series. You will need less time for this period than you did for the first half.

Conclusion

1. We began this study by examining Jesus' personality to discover how he is our prototype for both the developed ego and the Total Person (p. 171). As we close, describe Jesus as he has been revealed to you in this study as the individual who is an integrated person and a totally human being, living life completely, meeting the demands of both his inner and outer worlds. Has this description changed any from the one with which you started?

Sanford sums up the way Jesus is our prototype like this: "On the road to the Cross [Jesus] is the uniquely individual ego, made strong by consciousness and connection to God. Jesus, assuming the burden of crucifixion voluntarily and willingly, is the human ego at its prime, but on the Cross Jesus manifests more than the ego alone. Here he reveals totality, and is seen to be the 'Son of Man.' By his suffering, his death and resurrection, he merges forever with the human psyche, and shows himself the archetype of totality for all of us, transforming the destiny of humankind" (p. 171).

"Until Jesus' time psychological development was primarily accomplished on a collective basis. It was the herd, the group, the nation, the people, who were the bearers of human growth. Since Jesus, it has been the individual who carries forward human evolution, and the forward thrust of the creative life power, which is God's Holy Spirit in the world, takes place through the development of conscious life and the integration and completion of the total human being" (p. 172).

2. In light of the development that has taken place in you during this time, describe yourself, acknowledging your strengths and limitations, and outline a plan of action that would lead to an integration of the opposites within you.

Answers will vary. One or two participants might want to share their outlines for the benefit of those who are having a hard time imagining what to do.

Looking Ahead

Before the final closing, invite all to summarize their feelings about the time they have spent together. Ask for feedback from the group. It can be a simple word or phrase or it can be a longer statement acknowledging the value of the book, discussions, group process, personal insights. Let people say whatever they wish; encourage both negative and positive evaluation.

It would be advantageous for your work with future groups if you could elicit from this one how helpful, easy, or difficult it was to do the readings and assignments in preparation for each session. This is also one way to find out how seriously individuals took this study group.

Encourage them, in the future, to reread the book and the discussion guide questions to gauge their ongoing growth.

Also suggest that in time of prayer or reflection, they might reread the biblical selections that Sanford uses and identify the symbols (seed, fish, lightning, house, pearl, wedding, water, etc.) that say something to them. Indicate that by letting symbols speak to them they are in touch with the unconscious and creative parts of themselves.

Draw attention once more to their dreams and the importance of letting them speak of their unconscious needs. Encourage them to develop their own dream glossary using the explanations that Sanford gives in his dream analyses throughout the book.

Pass out the final handout, "Continuing the Learning," which outlines possible future activities for those interested in continuing what was begun in the group.

Closing

For the final service, you may need to allow more than ten minutes. Light the candle if it was not lit during the session. Ask all to pick up their symbols from the table and, one by one, to explain their significance. Be sure to bring one yourself and to participate in this process also.

After all have shared their symbols, have them place them on the table again. Form a circle around the table and hold hands to enclose them.

Ask those who wish to express a blessing. Suggest that everyone begin the blessing with the words, "I bless (or affirm) everyone here and ask for..." Model it by saying something like, "I bless everyone here and ask for continuing growth for each."

When this is finished, invite all to express their farewells in whatever way they wish.

Materials for Group Distribution

Glossary to Be Distributed Before Session 1

Glossary

Adversary: the person within us whom we perceive as our enemy since it is the one who contradicts the masks we present to others (p. 82).

Archetype: patterns which lie dormant in the unconscious until they are activated by our experience, models from which patterns of meaning develop as well as stimuli built into the brain which cause a person to behave in a certain way (p. 104).

Attitude: the posture or position one has towards life by which it is energized (the two psychological attitudes are extroversion and introversion).

Collective morality: a herd or split morality which encourages a positive attitude toward members of one's own group and a negative attitude toward nonmembers (p. 114).

Conscious: that part of our inner world which contains our personal experiences, memories, and data since conception.

Dark side of God: that aspect of God which allows crises and dark experiences to happen to people in order to call forth great inner strength and courage (p. 103).

Disciple: one who learns from the Master and follows the call to the individual way.

Dreams: those inner scenarios or dramas that we have while we sleep (p. 12).

Ego: the center of our conscious life and that part of our personality which we project to others (p. 12).

Ego-strength: the conscious personality that is capable of exerting itself effectively in life (pp. 22–23).

Eros: the power that binds together, unites, synthesizes and heals (p. 123).

Evaluation: objective appraisal of a person's character or personality.

Evil: a reality; an independent, autonomous agency opposed to God's will (pp. 98–109).

Extravert: one who finds the center of interest and sense of identity, appeal and value outside itself (p. 16).

This glossary may be photocopied for local use.

Glossary to Be Distributed Before Session 1

Faith: the capacity of a person to affirm life in spite of what life may bring, even in the face of doubts (pp. 118–36).

Feeling: the function of the human personality that is at home with feeling life and so is able to arrive at accurate and meaningful value judgments (p. 18).

Feminine aspect: comprises eros, or the capacity for relationships, understanding, awareness of others, receptiveness, creativity, patience, compassion, the valuing and nourishing of life, and an indirect way of attaining goals (pp. 21–22).

Function: the normal or proper activity of a person (p. 17).

Heart: a synonym for the unconscious.

Hubris: the insolence and arrogance caused by inordinate pride (p. 122n).

Hypocrite: a mask-wearer.

Individuation: the lifelong process of becoming the fully human beings we have been created to be.

Introvert: one who finds the center of interest and sense of identity, appeal, and value inside its inner world (p. 16).

Intuition: the function that "sees around corners" (p. 18).

Judging: determination, perseverance and enduring purpose.

Judgment: the process by which we condemn someone or something (pp. 90–91).

Masculine aspect: can be described as logos or reason and is lived out as active creativity, controlled agressiveness, psychological firmness, the capacity to strive for goals and overcome obstacles as these appear (pp. 21–22).

Mask: the person we pretend to be; the role we play in public (p. 70).

Myths: images which express the inexpressible.

Perceiving: apprehending, discerning, understanding.

Perfect: *not* a state of complete excellence—literally, "brought to an end state" (p. 95).

Pharisees: members of an ancient Jewish sect noted for the strict interpretation and observance of the written and oral law and for pretensions to superior sanctity. The Pharisees opposed Jesus because he stripped away their masks and revealed them for what they were.

This glossary may be photocopied for local use.

Glossary to Be Distributed Before Session 1

Projection: the process of ascribing one's own attitudes, feelings, values on to others as an unconscious defense against a sense of inadequacy or guilt (p. 84).

Prototype: the original or model on which something is formed; an archetype.

Psyche: a person's mental components, both conscious and unconscious; everything that is not physical (p. 17).

Self: a potentiality found in the core of one's being, the source of hidden possibilities, desires, aspirations, values, and attitudes (p. 101).

Sensation: that which has been called the "reality" function (p. 18).

Shadow: that hidden part of a person in the unconscious (p. 35). It contains the evil possibilities within us which can surface in dreams, fantasies, and symbols. It also contains the good possibilities which we may reject out of fear of the responsibilities that might be ours if we were to develop and use them.

Sin: to miss the mark (p. 111).

Soul: a psychic reality that makes one alive from within (pp. 118–36).

Symbol: an object which stands for something intangible.

Thinking: the function of the human personality that deals with situations by abstract thought or conceptualization and finds it difficult to deal with feeling (p. 18).

Transference: passing on forgotten childhood emotions to a person different from the one from whom they were initially experienced.

Unconscious: that personal layer of our inner world into which we store painful experiences and lost memories (p. 11).

This glossary may be photocopied for local use.

Bibliography to Be Distributed Before Session 1

Bibliography

Bradshaw, John. *Home Coming: Reclaiming and Championing Your Inner Child.* New York: Bantam Books, 1990. The author presents concepts, activities, and questionnaires that help to loosen the destructive hold of the past and awaken the healing potential of the inner Self.

Broyles, Anne. *Journaling: A Spirit Journey.* Nashville: Upper Room, 1988. Broyles explains how a journal chronicles a person's spiritual odyssey and provides six different methods for doing this successfully.

Caprio, Betsy. *The Woman Sealed in the Tower: A Psychological Approach to Feminine Spirituality.* New York: Paulist Press, 1982. By combining the psychology of Jung with the Christian tradition, Caprio explores both the "inner women" and the "inner men" found within women and shows how they can support or work against her.

Clift, Jean Dalby, and Wallace B. Clift. *Symbols of Transformation in Dreams.* New York: Crossroad, 1987. This is an innovative guide to understanding the messages which dreams bring us and which prod us toward wholeness. Illustrative dreams with their interpretations are included to show how these lead to transformation.

Johnson, Robert A. *We: Understanding the Psychology of Romantic Love.* San Francisco: Harper, 1983. If you have ever been in love or wished to be, *We* is a revealing account of the profound meaning of the experience; it is a map for the journey to greater consciousness.

Jung, Carl G. *Modern Man in Search of a Soul.* New York: Harcourt, Brace, Jovanovich, 1933. This book is an examination of the primitive unconscious, dreams, and the relationship between psychology and religion.

Kelsey, Morton. *Dreams: A Way to Listen to God.* New York: Paulist, 1978. The purpose of this book is to show accurately and simply how the ordinary person can begin to understand the varied and fascinating "shows" that take place in our psyches each night.

Lloyd, Roseann, and Richard Solly. *Journey Notes.* San Francisco: Harper, 1989. This tool for self-discovery covers the legacy of journal keeping, practical concerns of style, role playing, inner dialogues, affirmations, meditations, and other methods of writing.

This bibliography may be photocopied for local use.

Bibliography to Be Distributed Before Session 1

Menninger, Karl, M.D. *Whatever Became of Sin?* New York: Hawthorn Books, Inc., 1973. Menninger focuses on the moral sicknesses which afflict humankind. He acknowledges that there is such a thing as sin and that its consequences blur and diminish our lives.

Miller, William A. *Make Friends With Your Shadow.* Minneapolis: Augsburg, 1981. Miller deals with the dark, undesirable, potentially explosive side of personality called the "shadow" and urges the reader to make friends with it.

_____. *Your Golden Shadow.* San Francisco: Harper, 1989. This is a companion to *Make Friends With Your Shadow* and discusses the shadow's "golden side," the positive aspects of ourselves that we fail to see, accept, and develop.

Nelson, James B. *The Intimate Connection: Male Sexuality, Masculine Spirituality.* Philadelphia: Westminster, 1988. In light of the feminist revolution, Nelson explores the connection between male sexuality and masculine spirituality so as to understand the relationship to God, others, and the world.

Russell, Letty M. *Becoming Human.* Philadelphia: Westminster, 1982. In exploring what it means to be human, Russell focuses on who we are in light of Jesus' humanity, relationships between men and women, and how human liberation may be achieved.

Sanford, John A. *Dreams: God's Forgotten Language.* San Francisco: Harper, 1989. Beginning with the premise that dreams are fact and they exist, Sanford explores the relationship of dreams to religious experience.

_____. *Dreams and Healing.* New York: Paulist, 1978. In this volume, Sanford presents dreams as a wealth of creative possibilities, locked in the unconscious, on which we can draw when we learn to understand and relate them to our lives.

_____. *The Invisible Partners.* New York: Paulist, 1980. This book explores the masculine and feminine dimensions of the soul and demonstrates how the feminine part of a man and the masculine part of a woman are the invisible partners in a male-female relationship.

_____. *The Man Who Lost His Shadow.* New Jersey: Paulist, 1983. The author has written a modern variation of the Faust legend illuminated by insights from Jungian psychology. It points to the way people fail

This bibliography may be photocopied for local use.

Bibliography to Be Distributed Before Session 1

> to acknowledge the shadow side of their personalities and how that failure can lead to isolation and death.
>
> ———. *The Man Who Wrestled With God.* New York: Paulist, 1974. Using the stories of Jacob, Joseph, Moses, and Adam and Eve, Sanford illustrates individuation. He shows the importance of the process of intention, determined wrestling, resourcefulness, insight, and the circumstances of daily life as the ingredients for wholeness.

Savary, Louis M., et al. *Dreams and Spiritual Growth.* New York: Paulist, 1984. This book presents a comprehensive dreamwork methodology and integrates a psychological and spiritual approach to dreams and dreamwork.

Schaef, Anne Wilson. *Escape From Intimacy.* San Francisco: Harper, 1990. Focusing on relationship addiction, the author defines and contrasts the addictions of sex, love, and romance.

Whitehead, Evelyn Easton, and James D. Whitehead *A Sense of Sexuality: Christian Love and Intimacy.* New York: Doubleday, 1989. The Whiteheads explore a threefold yearning that people share: to rediscover the joy of sexuality as a gift without guilt; to accept an incarnational attitude toward intimacy; and to embrace the positive links between pleasure and commitment in Christian love.

This bibliography may be photocopied for local use.

Discussion Guide to Be Completed Before Session 1

Session 1: Getting to Know the Human Jesus

Read *The Kingdom Within,* introduction and chapter 1. Be aware that some words may be used differently from the way they are normally used. Sanford usually explains the Jungian terms, and the glossary can also help you. Bring up any terms you want to have clarified in the group.

Chapter 1: The Personality of Jesus

1. Identify the behavior within yourself that is extravert and introvert. Which predominates? What might be needed to bring a better balance to your life?

2. In light of what you know of Jesus, identify his extravert and introvert characteristics. What do these characteristics say about Jesus?

3. Do you feel you need to become better acquainted with Jesus? If so, how? Journal about the specific ways you can do this.

4. How was Jesus a thinking person, one who dealt with situations through abstract thought, arriving logically at a conclusion?

5. How was Jesus a feeling person, one who saw the value in a situation and then acted with compassion rather than judgment?

6. How was Jesus a sensate person, aware of facts through the senses and very practical about life?

7. How was Jesus an intuitive person, perceiving the subtle aspects of a relationship and of the possibilities in life?

This discussion guide may be photocopied for local use.

Closing Prayer to Be Distributed During Session 1

Closing Prayer: Session 1

Dear Lord,
I don't really know you.
It's true that I know a lot about you.
I have a lot of data and information.
I know who you are, what you have done.
In fact, I am awed by the magnificence of your
    works.
The seasons thunder your glory;
Living things mirror your creative imagination.
The handiworks of humankind reveal only a small
portion of the power and intelligence that you
    possess.

You have existed for an eternity,
    and yet this is only the beginning,
For infinity has no end;
    You are ever present.

I am afraid to make your acquaintance.
Getting to know you means I must recognize you
whenever you appear in another.
It means being open to the messages you dispatch
via whatever channel.
And it means welcoming and accepting the
    surprises of your kindness, your gentleness, your
care, your concern, your love for me, whenever
and however you send them.
It means scrambling through the pages of my
    personal history to comprehend how you have
impacted my story.

Knowing you means acknowledging you within
    me.
It means loving myself because you love me.
Fill me with knowledge of you, rather than
    knowledge about you,
For I truly yearn to get to know you.

Loretta Girzaitis

This prayer may be photocopied for local use.

Discussion Guide to Be Completed Before Session 2

Session 2: What Is Jesus Saying?

Read *The Kingdom Within*, chapters 2 and 3. Become acquainted with the meaning of *conscious, unconscious,* and *shadow,* as Sanford uses the words.

Chapter 2: The Treasure of the Kingdom of God

1. What is the treasure hidden within the field of your soul (Matt. 13:44)? What are you willing to give up to possess it? How are you a pearl found by the kingdom of God (Matt. 13:45–46)?

2. Searching and being sought are ongoing experiences and imply a continuing transformation of attitudes, values, and character. Draw a spiritual timeline and on it, identify the moments when such changes occurred in your life. Such a timeline highlights those periods in your life when some significant movement took place. Include those movements also where it seemed you may have backtracked or even moved away from God. Does any pattern emerge?

3. What does "being born again" (John 3:3) mean to you? How do you feel about Jesus' invitation to you for a special personal relationship with God?

4. Do you agree with the following statements? Indicate why or why not.

   A. Only the person who leads his or her life by an individually worked out set of values based on self-knowledge can enter the kingdom of God (Matt. 5:20).

   B. Lying within our shadow is the possibility of murder, adultery, stealing, lying, and coveting. For this reason the Law is necessary.

   C. When we confront and deal with the above possibilities, then we can live in love and transcend the Law (Matt. 5:17–18; Luke 16:17).

   D. When we obey the Law, we are better than prostitutes, murderers, drug addicts, alcoholics (Matt. 21:31).

This discussion guide may be photocopied for local use.

Discussion Guide to Be Completed Before Session 2

5. In one column list your inner values and in another your outer values (pp. 37–39). Then examine which rule your life and how these values support or negate one another. What do these insights say to you?

6. How does "understanding" the kingdom affect your life on earth? What does it promise after death? How do the present and future relate?

Chapter 3: Entering into the Kingdom

1. What does the saying "Many are called but few are chosen" (Matt. 22:14) mean to you? Would you consider yourself called and chosen or called and not chosen? Why must this be an individual decision?

2. Why do you agree or disagree with Sanford's statement that "people hate and fear individuality, with its demands for freedom and consciousness, and so they reject the kingdom of God" (p. 45)?

3. As you look at your life at this time, do you feel you are self-sufficient and can manage your life easily, or do you find yourself wounded, floundering, dissatisfied? Give an example from your experience to support your feeling. What do you need to do during this stage in your life?

4. Jesus said that people do not put new wine into old wineskins (Matt. 9:17; Mark 2:22; Luke 5:37–39). In your life, what corresponds to the old wineskin? the new wine? the new, fresh wineskin?

5. Visualize the story of the storm at sea as told in Luke 8:22–25. Think of an experience of yours that you connect with a storm at sea (or a hurricane), thunderous clouds (or driving rain), or an earthquake or tornado. Draw a picture of this symbol or write a poem connecting the symbol with your experience.

6. Choose one of these New Testament passages and write a short description of how it applies to your life: the narrow gate (Matt. 7:13); losing one's life (Matt. 10:31); the invitation to the wedding (Matt. 22:1–10; Luke 14:16–24); the house built on a rock (Matt. 7:24–25; Luke 6:47–48); or "Who do you say I am?" (Matt 16:13–20).

This discussion guide may be photocopied for local use.

Closing Prayer to Be Distributed During Session 2

Closing Prayer: Session 2

Decades ago, O Lord,
You designed a temple wherein to dwell.
Yet, I thought I knew better.
I built it my way and permitted
  rebellion to vandalize systematically,
    marring the exterior;
  anger to rampage wildly,
    ignoring the reckless damage;
  pride to scratch the interior,
    leaving its ugly graffiti;
  jealousy to blast its dynamite,
    collapsing this house built upon sand.

You study the rubble with compassionate eyes.
I sense the architect within you
  planning another blueprint.
Thank you for giving me another chance.
Help me to lay a new foundation
  of courage and of strength.
May I choose
  peace over rebellion,
  gentleness over pride,
  understanding over jealousy.
Fill this new temple with peace.
Help me to provide you with the space
  to expand the kingdom within me.

                              Loretta Girzaitis

This prayer may be photocopied for local use.

Discussion Guide to Be Completed Before Session 3

Session 3: Are We Willing to Pay the Price?

Read *The Kingdom Within,* chapters 4 and 5. If it would be helpful, find the verses mentioned in these chapters in your Bible in order to read them in their context.

Chapter 4: The Price of Discipleship

1. Sanford uses two New Testament images of Christ as the Word, one as a sword that divides and separates and the other as fire which burns and purifies (pp. 58–59). How relevant are these images to your life?

2. If you have separated from family identification, either inwardly or outwardly, how was this accomplished? Do you feel anything more has to be done?

3. Do you agree or disagree that our following of Christ aids us in establishing true relationships with others?

4. Sanford says, "The kingdom is not obedience, but creativity" (p. 66). What does this mean to you?

5. Jesus tells us that his yoke is easy and his burden light (Matt. 11:29–30) and he challenges us to accept them. Have you found this to be true in your experience? Why or why not?

6. Sanford emphasizes the need to move away from the group to foster individuality. What modern institutions and impulses contradict this? How do you deal with the apparent contradiction?

Chapter 5: The Pharisee in Each of Us

1. Recall a time when you wore your mask in a healthy way; in an unhealthy way.

2. Make two lists—one list for sins of the spirit, the other for sins of the flesh.

3. When have you acted as a "Pharisee"? What can you do to take your "heart" seriously?

This discussion guide may be photocopied for local use.

Discussion Guide to Be Completed Before Session 3

4. Read Psalm 139:1–18. Then write your own paraphrase of it. You might want to use the paraphrase in the handout as a model.

5. What is the ethic of the kingdom of God? What is the reality of living it out like for you?

6. Does Jesus condemn wealth in itself? How can wealth be an obstacle to the kingdom of God?

7. What does nakedness in dreams have to do with the nakedness in the Garden of Eden? What do you think of the quotation on page 78 from the Gospel According to Thomas?

8. At this time in your life, how can you shed your mask, that is, confront something in yourself that you do not like, even if it is unpleasant for you?

NOTE: Be alert to your dreams over a period of time and record them. Pay particular attention to those in which you may be fighting, disagreeing, or struggling with someone. Note what the quarreling is focusing on as well as with whom you are disagreeing. Is your adversary male or female?

Also record dreams where you are isolated or separated from others: walking on a lonely path; standing over an abyss; finding yourself at a fork in the road; struggling in a desert; lost in a jungle or wilderness. In addition, note dreams in which you are paralyzed when an animal or some threatening person is chasing you.

Write down the feelings you experienced in the dream and the ones you are experiencing as you write. What message(s) are these dreams sending you? Remember that the messages are related to whatever is happening in your life at the time of your dream. It would be helpful for you to share some or all of these dreams with someone who understands their language.

As you continue studying this book you will find Sanford referring to dreams. If you see dreams as an important way of getting to know your unconscious, then begin a glossary of symbols to which you can turn when you have dreams. Sanford explains the images clearly, so recognizing and understanding the symbols will be helpful in interpreting your own dreams.

This discussion guide may be photocopied for local use.

Closing Prayer to Be Distributed During Session 3

Closing Prayer: Session 3

A Paraphrase of Psalm 139

> My child, you are my beloved,
> and I know you intimately.
> I know your thoughts, desires, and feelings.
> I know your plans, dreams, and hopes.
> I have walked with you in your journey from your beginning,
> and I know what you can become in your future.
> Accept my presence and my love,
> for I will hold you up
> in all your moments of joy and of despair.
> Trust me, for I will scatter your darkness with my light.
> Before the seed was planted in your mother's womb,
> I knew you.
> I loved you and empowered you even then
> to be my witness.
> Believe that I will be with you
> even when you feel abandoned.
> I love you so much that I will guide you always
> until you have come home to me.
>
> Loretta Girzaitis

This prayer may be photocopied for local use.

Discussion Guide to Be Completed Before Session 4

Session 4: What Adversaries Block Our Path to God?

Read *The Kingdom Within,* chapters 6 and 7.

Chapter 6: The Inner Adversary

1. What kind of self-image do you have? How was it formed? What would happen to you if it were to change?

2. When are you aware of your inner adversary (p. 82)? How do you feel when it surfaces? What happens when you don't deal with it?

3. What happens when you identify and acknowledge the inner enemy as your own?

4. Do you agree with Sanford when he interprets the parable of the prodigal son as evidence of the two sides of our personalities (pp. 87–88)?

5. Can you identify any projections (p. 84) you have placed on others? What are the consequences both for you and for the other when this is done?

6. Make a list of your enemies. Alongside each name write down what you would need to do to make them your friends.

7. Rate yourself from 1 (not true) to 5 (true) on the inventory below by circling the number that applies for each statement. If you feel that some areas are important and need more attention, what steps can you take to make the statement a reality?

This inventory is personal and will not need to be shared with the group unless you care to identify some decision you are making because of the insights you gained as you did the inventory.

   A. I know and accept myself because I recognize that my past has shaped me into who I am today.

     1   2   3   4   5

   B. I acknowledge and embrace my inner enemy (shadow).

     1   2   3   4   5

This discussion guide may be photocopied for local use.

Discussion Guide to Be Completed Before Session 4

C. I identify and claim both my negative and positive feelings.

1   2   3   4   5

D. I live according to my inner values rather than those imposed from the outside.

1   2   3   4   5

E. I trust my intuition and God's grace that I can be "perfect," that I can become the person God has created me to become.

1   2   3   4   5

F. I believe that the kingdom can be established in me because my faults and failures contribute to developing my potential and capacity for love.

1   2   3   4   5

Chapter 7: The Role of Evil and Sin in the Way

1. Have you personally experienced crises that made you ask "Why?" Do you believe that evil experiences are allowed by the "dark side of God" (p. 103) so persons might achieve inner strength and courage?

2. Evil exists when something is not what it is meant to be. Since we are not whole (what we are meant to be), we are the prey of evil and so can possibly choose against God (p. 103). Identify as many areas of evil as you can: in the world; in others; in yourself.

3. Why is the ego important?

4. Sanford claims that the higher morality of love exceeds that of the Law, leading to a confrontation with this enemy (pp. 111–12). Would you be able to live without the Law and reach this higher plane? Why or why not?

5. As you read the following statements circle the letters (from strongly disagree to strongly agree) which identify your stance.

A. Guilt is healthy when it makes us conscious of our sinful behavior.

SD   D   N   A   SA

This discussion guide may be photocopied for local use.

Discussion Guide to Be Completed Before Session 4

B. It is necessary for us to be forgiven much, if we are to love much.

SD   D   N   A   SA

C. If we are to be united with God, we must drop our mask and consciously confront our inner enemy.

SD   D   N   A   SA

D. Sin is living unconsciously and when in sin it is not possible to make a free choice; we are thus enslaved to what we don't know about ourselves.

SD   D   N   A   SA

E. Only through consciousness can our inner divisions be brought within God's healing power.

SD   D   N   A   SA

6. Write two haiku poems—one on evil and one on sin. Haiku is a three-line poem with five syllables in the first line, seven in the second line, and five in the third line. Two poems are given as models.

> EVIL
>
> The demon within
> Defies God, claims my spirit,
> Makes itself my friend.
>
> SIN
>
> Darkness floods my heart.
> I flounder, lost in a maze,
> Choose what pleases me.

This discussion guide may be photocopied for local use.

Discussion Guide to Be Completed Before Session 5

Session 5: How Can We Live Life to the Fullest?

Read *The Kingdom Within*, chapters 8 and 9. As you study these chapters, choose one biblical verse that is significant for you. Prepare a short two- or three-sentence prayer or reflection to bring with you to the next session.

Chapter 8: The Faith of the Soul

1. Jesus was capable of lasting, deep, personal relationships because his eros (p. 123) was well developed. How are your relationships in light of your eros?

2. When Jesus speaks of faith, he is speaking of a certain capacity to affirm life in spite of what negatives life may bring. Is your faith deep enough to live life to its fullest?

3. Jesus asks "what does it profit a man if he gains the whole world and loses his soul." What would you be willing to give up to save your soul?

4. How conscious are you of your body, with its instincts and emotions? Do you honor, love, and care for it, or do you ignore, subdue, and/or chastise it?

5. How conscious are you of your soul, that reality that makes you alive from within? How do you nurture your relationship with it?

6. Write a letter to a person of the opposite sex in which you explain your feelings and values about these elements:

   A. the proper balance between repressing your sexuality and living it out promiscuously;

   B. the difference between the real person in your sexual life and the ideal person of your fantasies. What role does projection play in the latter?;

   C. the motivation(s) for a sexual experience with someone;

   D. the message that sexual fantasies have for you.

This discussion guide may be photocopied for local use.

Discussion Guide to Be Completed Before Session 5

You are writing this letter simply to clarify for yourself what your attitudes are about your own and others' bodies. There is no need to share this letter, unless you wish.

7. Do you agree that sexual sins are not as serious as hypocrisy, deceit, self-righteousness, egocentricity (p. 130)? Why or why not?

8. How conscious are you of your sexuality (your maleness or femaleness)? How and when do you express it and how does it affirm physical love and your respect for the other?

Chapter 9: The Lost Coin

1. Identify what you fear the most within yourself that you resist bringing into the light. How can you overcome this resistance?

2. In separate columns list the characteristics that you consider masculine and feminine. Put a check mark next to each characteristic that you feel is part of your personality.

3. In order to become a totally integrated and redeemed person, you need to find the lost sheep within you (Matt. 18:12–14; Luke 15:4–7). Who is your lost sheep?

4. In the parable of the lost coin (which is also the lost part of ourselves) we need to "light a lamp" (Luke 15:8–9) if we are to find that which is lost. On what do you need to shed the light of your mind and heart in order to search for and find your lost coin?

5. Jesus said, "I was hungry and you gave me food; I was thirsty and you gave me drink; I was a stranger and you made me welcome; naked and you clothed me, sick and you visited me, in prison and you came to see me. . . . I tell you solemnly, in so far as you did this to one of the least of these brothers of mine, you did it to me" (Matt. 25:35–36, 40). What is the naked, needy, hungry part of you that needs to be cared for? How can this inner beggar save you?

6. What sets us into position for receiving the kingdom of God?

This discussion guide may be photocopied for local use.

Discussion Guide to Be Completed Before Session 6

Session 6: How Is Jesus Our Mentor?

Read *The Kingdom Within*, chapter 10 and conclusion. You will need to bring a symbol to this session. This symbol is to identify you in some way. It may be something that you can find at home, or something from nature, or an object you may wish to purchase because it says something special about who you are.

You will also need to bring the drawing you made of your well. Reflect on the meaning of this well which is within you and the kind of living water that bubbles up and supplies you with energy. This reflection draws on your creative imagination.

Come prepared to evaluate this study group during session 6.

Chapter 10: The Coming of the Kingdom

1. The kingdom is established in our inner center when we surrender our ego to its supremacy. The paradox is that in this surrender the ego is strengthened and so becomes representative of our total personality. Read the sayings of Jesus in Matthew 10:39 and 23:12. Have you ever experienced this paradox in your outer life of commitment, or your inner life of surrender? If so, what resulted?

2. How does surrender differ from weakness?

3. Who are the poor in spirit? When do you see yourself as self-sufficient? as poor in spirit?

4. When are you childish (dependent, regressive, infantile)? When are you childlike (creative, spontaneous, free of inhibitions, generating new life)?

5. Read Isaiah 11:6–8. What is the wolf in you? the lamb? the panther? the kid? How can you take the hostile elements and make them friends with the gentle ones? How are you the little boy or little girl who leads them?

6. How prepared are you for your inner wedding (that union with Christ that brings freedom from evil because it is uniting the opposites within you [p. 153])?

This discussion guide may be photocopied for local use.

Discussion Guide to Be Completed Before Session 6

7. Why is it necessary that our inner journey be lifelong?

8. What connections can you make between creativity and fish?

Conclusion

1. We began this study by examining Jesus' personality to discover how he is our prototype for both the developed ego and the Total Person (p. 171). As we close, describe Jesus as he has been revealed to you in this study as the individual who is an integrated person and a totally human being, living life completely, meeting the demands of both his inner and outer worlds. Has this description changed any from the one with which you started?

2. In light of the development that has taken place in you during this time, describe yourself, acknowledging your strengths and limitations, and outline a plan of action that would lead to an integration of the opposites within you.

This discussion guide may be photocopied for local use.

Discussion Guide to Be Distributed During Session 6

Continuing the Learning

With this study, you have started a significant journey. Its continuation depends on your belief in its value, for that is what will determine how much time and interest you will expend on it. May you move forward, trusting that by activating your unconscious, you will discover the Christ-center within you. The kingdom of God will become your reality.

As time goes by, it is easy to forget that which seemed important at the time you were involved in it. So, to rekindle some of the enthusiasm, here are several suggestions that could be carried out over a period of time.

1. Locate the numerous Bible quotations that Sanford uses and reread his interpretations. Reflect on them so as to deepen their meaning for yourself. See if any personal insights surface as you become more familiar with the unconscious. Take your time with this and savor the quotations.

2. Pay special attention to the symbols described throughout the book, especially those connected with the Bible readings. Incorporate the meaningful ones into your life. For example, acknowledge and nurture the seed when it is planted within the soil of your heart. Or be consciously aware of drawing on your inner values rather than on those of authority figures, thus "leaving" your father and mother. Recognize the conflict between the younger and older brother within you.

As you allow your creativity to surface, you will become more aware of the symbolic in your life and will choose your own symbols to express your Self.

3. Locate the dreams that Sanford discusses. Study the symbols he describes and make your own dictionary. You can use it to study your own dreams. If you are interested in dreamwork, read the books on dreams listed in the bibliography and/or attend a dream workshop when it is offered in your area.

This discussion guide may be photocopied for local use.

Discussion Guide to Be Distributed During Session 6

4. Make a mandala. The mandala is a concentric design featuring a circular shape. By nature of its circular shape it suggests wholeness or totality. All points on a circle are equidistant from the center, and the circumference has no beginning nor end. It is appropriate for the mystery of the kingdom, since this perfect structure suggests the wholeness and harmony of the kingdom of God.

To form your mandala, make a large circle out of poster board. Fill it with pictures, words, symbols, and/or designs. These may be taken from magazines and newspapers, cut out in various shapes and pasted on the circle. Words and pictures can overlap and be placed in a variety of positions.

The mandala is to be a picture of yourself with your strengths and weaknesses and can be a reminder to you of those elements in your unconscious with which you must deal.

Some ways of forming the mandala might be: to put the conscious elements in the upper half and the unconscious elements in the lower half; or to put the strengths in the upper half and the weaknesses in the lower half; to work with the present and the future by placing "Who I Am" in the left half of the circle and "Who I Would Like to Become" in the right half. Or you could overlap both the strong and weak over one another. Use your creativity to design your mandala.

Do not rush. This may take weeks or months, but keep it in a place where you can work at it and where it would be a reminder of the kingdom of God that is possible within you. Upon completion, share it with a significant other person, maybe someone from this group with whom you have established a special relationship.

5. Periodically, get in touch with someone from this study group to check the progress on the action steps you set for yourselves throughout these sessions. Accountability to another frequently helps us to achieve our goals.

If you established rapport or a special friendship with a group member, you are fortunate, since support and understanding aid the process of discovering the kingdom, so nurture this relationship.

This discussion guide may be photocopied for local use.

Discussion Guide to Be Distributed During Session 6

6. The bibliography lists books that can add immeasurably to the knowledge you have gained so far. Choose books that are of particular interest and continue your development.

With this study, you have started a significant journey. Its continuation depends on your belief in its value, for that is what will determine how much time and interest you will expend on it. May you move forward, trusting that by activating your unconscious, you will discover the Christ-center within you. The kingdom of God will become your reality.

HAPPY JOURNEYING!

This discussion guide may be photocopied for local use.

Other Titles in Harper's Leader's Guide Series

The Coming of the Cosmic Christ by Matthew Fox
When the Heart Waits by Sue Monk Kidd
Addiction and Grace by Gerald G. May
Letters to Marc About Jesus by Henri J. M. Nouwen
Faith Under Fire by Daniel J. Simundson
Forgive and Forget by Lewis B. Smedes
A Tree Full of Angels by Macrina Wiederkehr

> You can order any of Harper's Leader's Guide Series books through your local bookstore or by writing to Torch Publishing Group, Harper San Francisco, 151 Union Street, Suite 401, San Francisco, CA 94111, or call us toll-free: 800-328-5125.